Alvin Harrington Low

Common Sense on Money

Alvin Harrington Low

Common Sense on Money

ISBN/EAN: 9783744721196

Printed in Europe, USA, Canada, Australia, Japan

Cover: Foto ©Suzi / pixelio.de

More available books at **www.hansebooks.com**

COMMON SENSE

ON MONEY.

By A. H. LOW.

THIRD EDITION.

NOTICE.

Any publisher desiring to copy any or all of this work will be granted the right to do so in writing, free, on application to me by letter, **on condition** that he shall publish one or more of the three divisions, i. e., the 100 paragraphs, the lecture or the dialogue **in full.** I make this condition to save from being misquoted and misunderstood. My object in copyrighting the work was to prevent its being garbled by my opponents.

A. H. LOW.

To Truth, Justice and Liberty, this little book is
most reverently dedicated.

—:o:——

CONTENTS.

PREFACE TO SECOND EDITION.

The rapid sale of the first edition has convinced the author that he has not mistaken the temper of the times.

This little book is not published in the interest of any political party, nor for the purpose of establishing a new party. The only motive is to promote the cause of Truth and Justice in relation to the most important of all national questions, *money*. Political parties are composed of the people, and unless the people are properly informed on national questions their representatives will not be. An American citizen has a double duty — that of *sovereign* and that of *subject*. Wholesome laws are the fruits of a wise exercise of sovereign authority. The power to make laws is the highest power which can be possessed by man. How important then that virtue and wisdom should temper the exercise of that power ! No political party embodies all the virtue and wisdom of a country. No one is wholly right — no one altogether wrong. The safety of the republic requires that there shall be more than one party. Absolute power is dangerous in the hands of any party as well as in the hands of any man. There are political parties enough in the United States to-day. If their leaders were all as zealous in emulating each other in good works as they are in vilifying one another, the land would soon resound with the glad shouts of happy workers, instead of echoing the groans of suffering and down-trampled millions. But to *do* right we must *know* the right; then, if we do it not, our sufferings will be but just penalties. For every evil, there is a vicious cause, and if we would remedy the evil, we must first find the cause, and then remove it. It is with the overwhelming conviction that the greater portion of the suffering and oppression experienced by the masses of the people of the United States, and especially of the laboring classes, is due to a vicious money system, (not so much in the quality as in the issue and control of the money,) and with the hope of shedding the light of Truth upon the subject, so that men of *every* political party can see their duty in relation to it, that the author has written this book. He believes that nearly every proposition stated herein, bears self-evident truth upon its face, and all are susceptible of overwhelming proof. Extensive quotation of authorities and exhaustive argument would

swell the book far beyond desirable and useful lim-
its. He contents himself therefore, with the rec-
ollection that " brevity is the soul of wit," and
that " enough is as good as a feast."

A. H. LOW.

COMMON SENSE ON MONEY.

—o—

1.   In every commercial country, art.ficiai facility for making exchanges is absolutely necessary.

2.   Man has invented money as a facility for making exchanges.

3.   Nothing is money until made so by man through his laws.

4.   The value of money determines the nominal value of everything for sale.

5.   Money is the measure of value.

6.   The measure of value *should be* as fixed and unchangeable as the measure of length or weight.

7.   How to establish a measure of value which will be fixed and unchangeable, has vexed the statesmen of ages.

8.   The variability in the standard measure of value, has wrought more injustice and suffering in the commercial world than all other causes combined.

9.   All money should be secure — a careful man would not go upon an unsafe bridge.

10.   Most commercial nations have tried to make gold the standard measure of value ; but gold varies in value, hence it is *not* an unvariable measure.

11.   All money to have actual value must be secured, for money is not security — it only *represents*
security.   The money of gold coin is secured by
and represents the gold in the coin ; the money of
a National bank-note is secured by U. S. bonds ;
U. S. bonds are secured by the honor and ability
of the United States to pay in gold or its equivalent in value.   Hence National bank-note money is
secured by, and represents value *not in it*. [See ¶ 53.]

12.   Gold and other coin, is prevented by law
from being used for other purposes than money,
while it is money; when used for anything else it
is not money, and paper money *cannot* be used for
anything else.

13. Something *must* and *does* determine the measure of the value of money as such, whether gold
or paper.   The *interest* which it draws does it.
[See ¶ 14.]

14.   The statement (paragraph 13) that interest
which it draws determines the measure of the value
of money as such, is based on the supposition that
the money is based on good security ; for if a certain amount of gold is a standard of security,
money which represents less in value, measured by
a full standard, than its nominal value indicates,
will be worth proportionately less in actual value,

than though it were fully secured and will be so much below par, and for this reason : The law of supply and demand operates to affect the current medium of exchange — money, *first*, by determining the commercial value of that which secures said money, as an article of commerce, and *secondly* as a medium of exchange — money. For example: The commercial value of gold as such, is regulated by the supply and demand of *gold* for its various uses. In this sense the value of a piece of gold is measured by the commodities for which it can be bartered. When the same piece of gold is coined into money, it is given a function or use which it did not before possess — that of money. And it is this new function that the interest it draws indicates the value of.

To make a just currency, its value as money and the value of its security must be maintained at the same degree.

15. For banking purposes, a dollar which will draw six per cent. interest is worth more than twice as much as a dollar which can draw only three per cent. interest.

16. All other things being equal, a dollar which will draw only two per cent. one day and will draw

six per cent. the next, is not an unvariable measure of value.

17. Interest measures the value of money, and
money the value of everything for sale. Hence a
change in the rate of interest changes the money
value of everything for sale.

18. Every one who sells anything for money, or
buys anything with money, uses the measure of
value every time he so sells or buys.

19. Every time the value of money is changed
by a change in the rate of interest it will draw,
the value of everything for sale is changed *inversely*.
If money costs more, (draws higher interest,) other
things sell for less, and when money costs less,
(draws lower interest,) other things sell for more.

20. Congress has the power, and it is its *duty* to
regulate and *fix* the value of money, as well as to
fix the standard of weights and measures. [See
Const. U. S., Art. 1, Sec. 8.]

21. Congress has never *fixed* the value of money.

22. Congress has attempted to *regulate* the value
of money by fixing the *maximum* rate of interest
to be *legally* charged by the National Banking Associations, while no *minimum* is fixed. Hence the
value of money is not fixed. [See ¶ 43.]

23. Suppose Congress should say " the yard shall

never be more than three feet long, but it may be less," would the yard measure be fixed? No.

24. Suppose Congress should say to a corporation, "we give you, exclusively, the yard-stick ; it shall be the standard measure of length through- the country ; you shall not increase its length, but you may diminish it whenever it can be done to your advantage," would not the measure of all property to be measured by the yard be subjected to the caprice of that corporation ? Congress *has done* as much with money.

25. If I have a farm worth $1,000 which will pay me a net yearly profit of $70, and for that rea- son the government freely enables me exclusively to lend my note for $900, and I do it and receive $63 as interest for the use of it the same year, has not the government increased my wealth $63 with- out a consideration ? Yes. The government does as much for the bondholders — the National Bank- ing Associations.

26. The "National Banking System" has one good feature that the old banking system did not have — the payment of National Bank Notes is se- cured. [See ¶ 82.]

27. The evils and injustice resulting from the

old and the present banking systems are beyond computation for magnitude.

28. Congress has bestowed on the owners of United States bonds, this great exclusive grant over all other people — *it has made their notes money.* Who but a National Banking Association can *pay* his debts to another by giving his own note?

29. If I owe a debt which must be paid in money, *my* note, however well secured, will not pay it.

30. Except the metal money, "greenbacks" and Treasury certificates, the National Banking Associations provide all the money, and may provide little or much at their pleasure.

31. The National Banking Associations are only limited in the amount of the notes they can issue by the amount of the United States bonds in existence, and the people's need of facility for making exchanges. They can go no farther that way ; but may go the other way to nothing.

32. One great wrong of the "National Banking System" is, that the government endorses and makes money of the notes of *one class*, who can put up a certain kind of security, exclusively.

33. The National Banking Association, by having the power to increase or diminish the facility

(money) for making exchanges, have the control of the measure of value in this country. They may enlarge it by contracting and charging more interest, and diminish it by expanding and charging less, — *and they do !*

34. While the present (A. D. 1883) banking system exists, the measures of value can never be *fixed* **and** safe.

35. A commercial country and its money are in many respects like a man's body and blood; when the money is all concentrated in the banks of the " money centres " the country at large feels the loss of the vital current of commerce, and all business is chilled and depressed. So with a man, when there is a congestion of blood about the heart and suffocation there, all the extremities of the body are cold and numb. Start the current in either case — drive the life-blood out into the body or supply sufficient money to the country, and health and activity are restored. Again if the blood in the human body is corrupted — becomes watered or otherwise reduced below the natural standard, disease to the whole system follows. Corrupt the money of a country — make some poorer than the rest or change its quality of a stable standard

measure of value, and the whole economy of commerce is deranged.

36. A "money market" ought to be an impossibility. Going to the money market and paying the extortioner's price for money is like putting mustard draughts on the feet to get up a circulation. The very act pre-supposes a disease. The idea of a market carries with it the idea of variation in price.

37. No one can afford to pay as great a price for a thing with money which he has borrowed, or could lend at seven per cent., as he could at one per cent., and this is why the interest on money governs the prices of things.

38. The *intrinsic* value of things does not fluctuate with the rate of interest on money — it is their nominal or selling price or value which fluctuates.

39. The nominal value of all property does not fluctuate simultaneously with the rate of interest. It takes time for the sound of a blow to reach the ear.

40. Whatever power, whether of person, corporation, or nation, that can expand and contract the volume of the medium of exchange, may diminish or increase the price of all articles for sale,

and does so whenever such expansion or contraction is made, where there is no fixed, permanent rate of interest. The National Banking Associations have the sole power over the volume of money in the United States. They may deposit United States bonds and increase their notes without limit (except the limited amount of United States bonds), and may call in and surrender their notes and take up their bonds.

41. The only motive for the expansion and contraction of the medium of exchange is *gain* — gain to those who cause the change. Interest is the gain to banking associations.

42. By combining, the National Banking Associations can, in a short time, gather in and hold all the money in the country, and then demand, and receive, the highest rate of interest allowed by law for loans, and continue to do so until a sufficient volume for making exchanges is supplied. Then by refusing to loan, and forcing payment of their creditors, again collect in and withhold all the money, when the operation may be repeated. Is not the National Banking System a national devil-fish?

43. The Government has made 23.22 grains of pure gold coined into a dollar-piece of 25.8 grains,

the unit of value : but it has left the value of that unit uncertain. It should make it certain by fixing the rate of interest it shall draw when loaned. [See ¶ 22.] Prior to 1873 the silver dollar was the unit of value. It answered the purpose very well and might do so again, with proper laws, *regulating its value*

44. When the money is all out, the money-lenders can sell their property at good prices — when it is all in they can buy it back at reduced prices.

45. By co-operation for mutual advantage, of the National Banking Associations and other money lenders, (brokers, etc.,) the former may decline to loan to the people generally, but loan to the latter at the full legal rate of interest, and they, in turn, lend to the people at higher rates, thus demanding the " pound of flesh."

46. The exorbitant compensation the people pay the National Banking Associations for their services is the least of the evils attending the National Banking System. *They may increase or diminish the measure of value at will.*

47. All the interest paid to bankers and brokers for the use of money, in excess of the cost of making and issuing said money, and the trifling tax

they pay on their business, is extorted from the people by the laws made by the people's representatives.

48.　If bankers make an unjust profit (and what one does not?) the people must lose to an equal amount.　Bankers as such have been non-producers, except of want and misery to others !

49.　*Interest* is the banker's income, and the gauge by which the value of money is determined.

50.　Money is the measure of the value of all things *for sale or saleable.*　There are things the value of which it does not measure as air, water, sunlight, etc.

51.　All the consideration the National Banking Associations give in return for their exclusive rights, is the small tax they pay the Government and the cost of making and loaning their notes. If this could be done by the Government, *they* are not needed.

52.　This difference exists between my note and that of the National Banking Associations. I *pay* interest on my note, and *they draw* interest on theirs.

53.　The currency of money depends upon the security which it represents.　Hence all *current* money must be *secured* by something. [See ¶ 11.]

54. Silver and the base metal coins do not *contain* the amount of security that gold coin does, yet they are current for their full face value. Why? Because the government has issued them for their face value and made them redeemable or convertible for their face value in gold. When presented in certain sums, the government redeems them at their face value, just as much as it does a Treasury note. In other words, silver and the base-metal coin money represents the metal in it for part of its face value and the *honor* and *ability* of the nation to pay for the balance. So all the talk about silver and the minor coins being "the money of the poor" is unfounded; at least those words have been used to convey a false idea.

55. The present money system is vicious and oppressive to all but the one favored class. This wrong we, the people, through our representatives, have done ourselves, and we alone can and must repair it.

56. If justice prevailed among men, and all were happy, no reforms would be sought or needed.

57. All reforms are inaugurated by the sufferers from the wrong sought to be overcome.

58. They who profit by wrong never seek its overthrow — their interests point the other way.

59. If the money-lenders have an undue and unjust advantage of the rest of the community the sufferers must right the wrong — the others never will.

60. The ballot is the weapon with which Americans should right their wrongs.

61. Complaining of evils for which we offer no remedy, is a weak occupation.

62. The necessity for a measure of value is universally admitted, and it is a self-evident truth that the measure should be standard, unvariable and fixed.

63. The statesmen (?) of this country have selected gold as the material best suited for a standard of value. They have never *fixed its* value, hence they have never fixed the standard of value.

64. Value is not matter. Can we then measure value with matter?

65. Gold is not value; it is substance. The value of gold is its use, and so with all other substances. But use is not matter or substance. Then, if the value of gold is its use, its use measures the value of gold, and having thus determined the value of a quantity of gold as money, we may *fix* it

as a standard, and by that standard measure the value of all other things for sale. [See ¶ 72.]

66. There is no fixed, unvariable standard measure of value in this country. No, not in the world, to-day ! We must provide such a standard, or suffer a thousand times more than we now do, for this is a new country, and wealth is not centralized as in older countries, but it soon will be if we do not awake !

67. We, the Government, take the bonds which we have given, as security, and thereupon make the notes of the pledgeors money. Is no other property as good security as the bonds we have given ? Is not land ? The banks take it and many other things as well.

68. The Government can issue its own notes equal to gold in value, as in case of the present "greenbacks" but *only to a limited extent*, without additional security. The extent to which it may do so depends upon its revenues and sales of lands, etc., for upon these depends its *ability* to pay or redeem them.

69. Why could not and should not the Government take security similar to that which the banks take, and lend its notes and make those notes money ?

70. With the gold dollar as a standard measure of value, all other money should be secured by and represent *something* of the value of gold, of its nominal — its declared value. So all money should be equal in measuring values.

71. With gold money as a standard, the security of money does not affect the *value* of money when it is at or above par with gold. That is, if paper money is so secured that it is at par with gold no additional security can make it at a premium. Its *convenience* over gold may slightly increase its value, but its security does not.

72. Money is worthless if it cannot be used. Hence the use of money is all that gives it its value. The power to use money is created by the Government, or law. If the Government can create the power to use money, may it not limit its use? Yes, it may do that by establishing a fixed, unvariable rate of interest. [See ¶ 65.]

73. As matter acted upon by the law of God for that purpose, becomes a living soul, so matter, acted upon by the law of man for that purpose, becomes money.

74. If Government makes money which is not secured in *some way*, it will not be used as a medi-

um of exchange. Government makes money by law, but it cannot force its use.

75. Honor, alone, can never be good security, nor any, for the payment of money. It must be coupled with *ability* to pay.

76. It is the *honor* and *ability* of a nation that imparts value to its promises to pay. These together form the security upon which its promises rest, and depend for their value.

77. A nation's notes or promises to pay money, differ from private individual promises to pay, in this: If the nation refuse to pay, the creditor has no means by which to force payment ; but, through the law, the creditor of a private debtor may force payment.

78. Inflation of the current money in the country, if it be all well secured equal with the security of gold money, works evil only through the rate of interest it bears, and if there was but one rate of interest established, too much money could not be.

79. There is a great advantage in paper money over metal money, in this: while the paper answers every purpose as money that metal does, the substance which the paper money represents and upon which it is dependent for its value, may be produc-

tive and useful for other purposes ; whereas, the substance of metal money, upon which its value wholly or largely depends, can only be used as *money* while it is money. Hence gold, silver, etc., are an expensive currency.

80. Money is purely a facility for making exchanges. Can there be too much facility for doing a lawful and laudable act ?

81. All money should be full legal tender in payment of all debts payable in money.

82. The holders of U. S. bonds have, unwittingly, done one thing for which we might be thankful ; they have shown us how good paper money may be made. They did not think when they were influencing our representatives to pass the banking laws, for their exclusive use, that their patent could ever expire. But it will ! [See ¶ 26.]

83. Gold, of a certain weight and fineness, is a good material out of which to form the standard measure of value. Then fix the money value of *that* by fixing the rate of interest it may draw, and you will have a standard measure of value as fixed and certain as a straight piece of wood exactly three feet long, well preserved, and made by law the standard measure of length, would be a fixed and certain measure of length.

84. We propose then, as a remedy for the evil which we complain of, that the Government make its notes and lend them to all who apply, and give good and sufficient security therefor, at a certain annual rate of interest and for so long a time as the borrower desires and pays the interest promptly when due, and the security holds good ; that it make said notes a legal tender for the payment of all debts payable in money, when no kind of money is expressly specified in the contract ; that it establish and fix said rate of interest as the legal rate of interest throughout the country, and provide by law that whoever lends money for a higher or lower rate of interest shall forfeit the whole sum he has so loaned, to the one to whom he has loaned it ; and that it make no more National bank-notes money.

85. To give currency to a note issued by the government, it is not necessary that it shall be expressly or impliedly a promise to pay in coin. That would be a practical falsehood upon its face, taking all the coin and all the paper money together. *If the gold dollar is retained as the unit of value*, the promise should be " The United States of America will pay to Bearer .... Dollars on demand, in gold money or its equivalent in

value in lawful money of the United States," and this note should be declared lawful money and a full legal tender in payment of all debts public and private, when no other money is expresslv specified by contract. Thus the Government would agree to maintain its credit at par with the unit of value.

86. If men cry out, " this will ruin all banking business !'' to them we will answer, "it will break up the dens of thieves !''

87. If men ask " what will the ' capitalists ' and bankers do with their money ?'' we answer, " they will lend it at the same rate of interest that the people, through their government, do, or buy property with it, which they can use or else lay out of the use of their money as other people do !''

88. We do not propose to take away the property of any one without a consideration for it ; we do propose to withhold further bestowal of our bounty where it is not deserved.

89. With an established, fixed, and unvariable rate of interest, there would be no motive for hoarding money. Then money would always seek investment instead of investment seeking money as now.

90. The holders of U. S. bonds have been protected in the exclusive right and use of their inven-

tion, the National Banking System, for over nine-teen years — longer than patents on other inventions run. They have abused their privileges and their patent ought to be cancelled.

91. We do not propose to annul the National bank charters as a necessity. Let them compete with the government in bestowing benefits upon the people ; but stop making their notes money.

92. If the Government changes the rate of interest in establishing our system, let Congress pass a law providing that the consideration of all contracts for payment of money, made prior to the time the reform goes into effect, and in which contracts the value of money to be paid is not specified, shall be paid in money of equal value to the value of the amount of money agreed to be paid was at the time the contract was made. Then no injustice can be done by the change. This would not be a law impairing the spirit of the obligation of contracts.

93. Every time the National Banking Associations change the rate of interest they impair not the letter, but the spirit of the obligation of contracts.

94. The Government ought to establish a cen-

tral bank with branches all over the country. wherever needed by the people.

95. It will cost no more to run the Government banks than it does the " National Banks " and the profits will go into the U. S. Treasury where they belong.

96. The Government issues money secured by gold and silver (the security of gold money is in the coin itself,) why should not it make and issue money on other security *not in it?* It should ! It does so in case of the present National Bank notes. Why not in case of other notes ? What gives gold, silver, government bonds, or the nation's credit a right to preference over all other property for security ?

97. The vital interest and welfare of every man, woman and child, of every farmer, trader, manufacturer and merchant, of every laborer, mechanic, teacher, writer, and publisher, of *everybody except the money lender*, will be secured and improved by the establishment of the banking system herein proposed.

98. The plan proposed in this book is as adaptable to every other nation on earth as it is to ours.

99. The bondholders, their hirelings, and their

blind followers, will cry out against this reform, saying "it is revolution!" Yes, we admit it — it is revolution from chaos to order !

100. On the establishment of a just money system depends the perpetuity of the Republic. Personal interest is the motive power of commerce. It is for the people to determine whether the personal interests of a few who issue a large portion of the money of this country shall be the gauge by which the commerce of the country shall be governed, or whether the personal interest of every individual under the Government shall be consulted. With such an issue, it seems impossible that the matter can remain long undecided. Can any one deny that such an issue really exists ? Until he can reveal something besides the personal private interest of the National Banking Associations that induces them to issue their notes and to expand or contract the currency, his denial is but empty words.

Does it ever occur that the whole country is in trouble for want of postal facilities ? Surely not. Why ? Because the system is managed by the people through their servants for the interests of all. Our money system should be conducted in the same way. Some object, that it would be too great an undertaking for the Government to manage the loaning of money or, as they put it, go into the banking business. This is the most forcible objection that can be produced but it has no rational foundation. If the good of all the people demands it ; if justice demands it ; if national life demands it ; if human liberty demands it, nothing is too great for Government to undertake. Government is instituted for the benefit of the governed ; when it falls short of this, government is worse than useless. The battle of life is an unequal contest at best, and it is to restrain the strong from undue aggression upon the rights of the weak that many laws are necessary. How vicious then is a law which gives to the strong new advantages over the weak ! Such is a law that gives to private persons or corporations the power to furnish a country with money, with no restraint except the personal interests of those persons or corporations. Such is the state of things in the United States to-day. Any government that strengthens the hands of the strong against the weak — the few against the many, is a despotism whether in name it be democracy, republic or monarchy.

No despotism was ever more far-reaching and unjust than that of the money power of this country. I do not assail the men who have money and those who issue it as possessed of more wicked and cruel hearts than the rest of us. Personal interest is the tyrant in them as it would be in us if we were in their places. What I assail is the policy of government that fosters the personal interests of a few to the injury of all the rest. Such has been and is the policy of this Government. While we preserve the forms of representative government we are actually ruled by a moneyed oligarchy. We may congratulate ourselves that we have still the recognized right to shape the legislation of this country. Will we content ourselves with the possession of that right and not exercise it ?

We have the choice between sovereignty and slavery. The prerogative of sovereignty will be exercised in this country. It is for us to say whether we as a people shall exercise it, or delegate it to others to be used for their advantage and our ruin. It is our duty and it is for our interest to lay aside party fealty and party prejudice and unite as one man in the work of electing a Congress that will be loyal to their sovereign, and enact such laws as shall preserve equal justice to all the people.

APPENDIX.

———o———

The author respectfully submits the following quotations, in support of some of the ideas advanced in this book.

At this very time, (about 1770) even the silver money in England is obliged to the legal tender for a part of its value. BENJAMIN FRANKLIN.

———

Bank paper must be suppressed, and the circulating medium must be restored to the Nation to whom it belongs . . . . . . It is literally true that the toleration of banks of paper discount, costs the United States one half of their war taxes, or in other words, doubles the expenses of every war. THOMAS JEFFERSON in 1813.

———

It is however, essential to every modification of the finances that the benefits of a uniform national currency should be restored to the community . . . . . . There is only wanting to the fiscal prosperity of the Government the restoration of a uniform medium of exchange . . . . . . For the interests of the community at-large as well as for the purposes of the Treasury, it is essential that the Nation should possess a currency of equal value credit and use, wherever it may circulate. The Constitution has intrusted Congress exclusively with the power of creating and regulating a currency of that description. JAMES MADISON in 1815-1816.

———

A bank of the United States is, in many respects, convenient for the Government and useful to the people . . . . That a bank of the United States competent to do all the duties which may be required by the Government, might be so organized as not to infringe on our own delegated powers, or the reserved rights of the States, I do not entertain a doubt.

ANDREW JACKSON in 1832.

———

When to this it is added, that the bills are not only receivable everywhere in Government dues, but that the Government itself would be bound for their ultimate redemption, no rational doubt can exist, that the paper which the exchequer would furnish, would readily enter into general circulation, and be maintained at all times at or above par with gold and silver, thereby realizing the great want of the age and fulfilling the wishes of the people . . . . . The whole matter of the currency would have been placed where by the Consitution it was designed to be placed — under the immediate supervision and control of Congress . . . . . . The same eye which rests unceasingly on the specie currency, and guards it against adulteration, would also have rested on the paper currency, to control and regulate its issue and protect it against depreciation. The same reason which would forbid Congress from parting with the power over the coinage would seem to operate with nearly equal force in regard to any substitution for the precious metals in the form of a circulating medium.

JOHN TYLER, in 1841 and 1843.

———

The Government ought not to delegate this power if it could. It was too great a power to be trusted to any banking company whatever, or to any authority but the highest and most responsible which was known to our form of Government . . . . . . The Government itself ceases to be independent; it ceases to be safe when the national currency is at the will of a company . . . . . All property is at their mercy. The price of real estate, of every growing crop, of every staple article in the market, is at their command. Stocks are their playthings — their gambling theatre, on which they gamble daily with as little secrecy and as little morality, and far more mischief to fortunes than common gamblers carry on their operations.

Thos. H. Benton, U. S. S. about 1838.

———

Congress, as the Legislature of a sovereign nation, being expressly empowered by the Constitution " to lay and collect taxes, to pay debts, and to provide for the common defence and general welfare of the United States," and " to borrow money on the credit of the United States " and to coin money and regulate the value thereof and of foreign coin," and being clearly authorized, as incidental to the exercise of those great powers to emit bills of credit, to charter national banks, and to provide a national currency for the whole people, in the form of coin, Treasury notes, and National bank bills, and the power to make the notes of the Government a legal tender in payment of private debts, being one of the powers belonging to sovereignty in other civilized nations, and not expressly withheld from Congress by the Constitution, we are irresistibly impelled to the conclusion that the impressing upon the Treasury notes of the United States, the quality of being a legal tender in payment of private debts, is an appropriate means, conducive and plainly adapted to the execution of the undoubted powers of Congress, consistent with the letter and spirit of the Constitution, and therefore, within the meaning of that instrument " necessary and proper for carrying into execution the powers vested by this Constitution in the government of the United States." Such being our conclusion in matter of law, the question whether at any particular time, in war or in peace, the exigency is such by reason of unusual and pressing demands on the resources of the government, or of the inadequacy of the supply of gold and silver coin to furnish the currency needed for the uses of the government, and of the people, that it is, as matter of fact, wise and expedient to resort to this means is a political question to be determined by Congress, when the question of exigency arises, and not a judicial question to be afterward passed upon by the Courts.

Extract from opinion of U. S. Supreme Court, in case of Juilliard vs. Greenman.

VALUES AND MONEY.

A LECTURE BY A. H. LOW.

A theory to be worthy of notice must be founded upon one or more facts. The comparison of wisdom of two men, the one of whom built his house upon the sand and the other who built his upon the rock, is parallel to that of a man who founds his theories upon imaginary existence of a thing and one who founds his upon the thing itself. Now there are two kinds of facts — facts that are self-evident or such as require no argument to make them believed or understood, and facts that are so concealed from view by the interposition of other facts that they cannot be seen at once, but must be first uncovered and stripped of their surroundings before they can be recognized.

It is my purpose here to call attention to certain elements, which go to make up value ; to determine what is value, and distinguish between value in the abstract and commercial value — to show how value is attached to money and how it may be limited there so as to make the value of money an unvariable measure of the value of all things for sale.

Webster defines value to be : the property or

properties of a thing which render it useful ; or the degree of such property or properties. As familiar objects possessing value to mankind, I will mention air, water, light of the sun, etc. These are things of inestimable value to man because his very existence depends upon them. Deprive him of either of these and he cannot live. Yet I have seen it laid down as a fact in a book in use in our common schools that air has no value because it is unlimited in supply ! If value is the property or properties of a thing which render it useful, I hold it to be self-evident that usefulness determines its value, and degree of usefulness, its degree of value.

There are things which are useful to man yet not indispensable. A horse, carriage, steam-engine, sail-vessel or money, are of the things useful to man, for each and all may add to his happiness and comfort, yet they are none of them indispensable to him, for he may live and be comfortable and happy without them.

It is evident then, that those things which are of most value to us are most bountifully provided and cost us least to obtain.

But the Creator has so formed us and surrounded us with such conditions that but few things which go to make up the sum even of our needs, and much less our wants, are at our disposal except on condition that we put forth our own efforts and labors to obtain them, and it is from this fact that has arisen the distinction of values, or the abstract, intrinsic value of things and the commercial value of things.

If each individual by his own exertions procured from nature only what his necessities demanded, there could be no commerce in products, and were each individual able to so procure all his necessities and wants demanded, there would be no need of commerce in products, but mankind as a whole is so fashioned that no one without the assistance of the rest can provide himself with even the absolute necessaries of life. We are created with diverse talents and abilities, and it is from these characteristics of man that commerce in commodities or products arises. We may say then that commerce in commodities is a providential necessity. Yet commerce is the *work* of man. The Creator made man ; imposed on him the necessity of exertion to the end that he might live, and endowed him with the talents necessary for the accomplishment of that end, and commerce is the institution of man arising out of those necessities and the exercise of those talents.

All writers on history or political economy agree, that the commerce of the world to-day is immensely more adapted to the wants of man than that of even a thousand years ago, and that the machinery of commerce has been undergoing improvement and change since the advent of man, to suit the demands of his improved state of developement in civilization and enlightenment. It is also generally agreed, that the first stage of commerce consisted of barter, or the exchange of one thing of use and limited in supply for another, also of use and limited in supply. As for example, where A. who had raised or obtained more wheat than he needed, exchanged his surplus for meat of which he had not sufficient with B. who had procured more meat than he needed, who exchanged his surplus of meat for A.'s surplus of wheat which he needed. Yet exchange is the basis of commerce. Nay, it is commerce itself.

At this stage of commerce, it requires no great play of the imagination to see the cumbersome working of the machinery, and that it might occur that a man might be compelled to make many exchanges before he parted with all his surplus for what would supply his needs. He must seek another one who wanted what he had and had what he wanted, and that in just the right proportion, or he must part with what he did not want, for other things he did not want thereby to increase his variety of articles in hopes of being able the better to exchange for what he did want, and in the right proportion. But this was not his only difficulty, everything that man produced which was of use had a value. That value was in degree equal to its supply and use, and its commercial value was determined by its supply and its demand for use. Observe now that I say *demand* for use. A thing may be useful in itself, but if that usefulness is not known to man, there will be no demand for it, Hence when we speak of commercial value, we mean the property or properties of a useful thing of limited supply and in demand, or that the value of the thing is governed by the law of supply and demand.

In the absence of a standard measure of value it was difficult if not impossible to determine when an exchange was made, whether it was made on just and equitable terms or not. How was A. who had a measure of wheat to exchange for salt, to know how many measures of salt he should receive for it?

Now the exponent of one class of political economists will reply, " he will calculate the number of days' labor each cost and judge by that.'' But suppose that the amount of labor each article cost was to be the standard of value and one article was in greater demand for use than the other, would labor be a just standard then ? Suppose again that the salt manufacturer had expended his labor with wisdom, obtaining thereby the greatest returns for his. exertions, and the wheat producer had foolishly done all his work the hardest way, thereby receiving the smallest returns for it, would the days' labor then be a fair standard of the value of their products, and if so, the labor of which will we take for the standard ? And if you say neither but the average of both, how shall we determine that average? To extricate commerce from the embarrassment here disclosed, man could not have been long in devising something to act as a measure of value, and it is interesting to note what a variety of things have been adopted for that purpose ; for history tells us, that animals, the barks of trees, leather, iron, tobacco, copper, shells, silver, gold, paper, and almost everything known to commerce, has at one time or another been used as a standard of value, under the general name of money.

Why has there been so much experimenting in

this matter of a standard measure of value? — But
here another philosopher calls me to order by
denying that money is the measure of value! If
not, what is? I agree that it is not and never has
been a just, unvariable measure of value, but it is,
and has been the only measure of value for things
saleable or for sale that man has ever invented.
Take a single instance for illustration : A. has
more butter than he needs and less sugar ; B. has
more sugar and less butter ; A. does not go to B. un-
informed of the market price of butter and sugar
and propose an exchange of his butter for B.'s sugar, weight for weight, but he ascertains how much
money his butter and B.'s sugar are worth per
pound, and then if more convenient to exchange
with B. than to sell his butter in the market for
the money and afterwards go to B. with the pro-
ceeds of his butter in money, he says to B. " butter is worth so much money per pound, and I
learn that sugar is worth so much per pound in money. Then they ascertain the money value of each lot
by multiplying the price per pound by the number of
pounds and make their exchange upon the basis
of the values so ascertained. Then, since the value
of each article has been compared with the value
of money, and the exchange made according to

the result of that comparison, has not the value of the money acted as the measure of the value of each? But money, although it has always been used as a measure of value, has itself been of uncertain value. We have seen that a thing to be of value must be of use. That to be of commercial value it must be limited in supply as well as to be of use. It follows that, with a given supply, an increase or decline in demand increases or lessens the commercial value, and with a given demand an increase or decline in supply lessens or increases the commercial value.

And now I am ready to, and do assert that the same rule applies to money, with the same force that it does to all other articles of commerce, and it is from this fact, that money as it has been and is, is not an unvariable measure of value We must not confound the value of money, with the thing money. Money may have a nominal value and yet not be current in commerce for want of actual value. Money can be used as a measure of value, (however imperfectly) while it has or represents value, but when it becomes valueless, it is useless as a measure.

Money may be established in two ways : — By common consent and usage among the people, or by law enacted by or through the sovereign power in a State or nation. Whatever is used as a standard measure of commercial value, and a medium of exchange, is money in essence whether it be so in name or not. So it is not the material of which it is composed but the functions which it possesses that makes it money, and since it is the law merchant or law statute that confers upon it these functions, we say law makes the money. It is from this fact that many have concluded that statute law also gives money all its value. I believe I shall be able to show that this is a mistaken theory. I think I have shown you that there is an inexorable law which governs commercial values — the law of supply and demand — and that money is subject to that law. I will give you the key to that law : it is personal interest. Personal interest is the motive power of commerce. Take from it this element, and you rob it of its very life.

But money is not only a measure of value, but it is a medium of exchange. It may perform the functions of a measure of value, by comparison, without acting as a medium of exchange — for it acts as a medium of exchange only when it is itself exchanged for something else. The money in this country does not change hands, nor any portion of it, every time an exchange of commodities is made. Yet every exchange of commodities is made by comparing the values of those commodities with the value of money.

I will not insult your intelligence by entering upon an elaborate explanation of how money acts as a medium of exchange. Its necessity for that purpose and its function of such a medium are self-evident to us all.

It is less evident however, what gives money its value. But we have already seen that all commercial values are governed by supply and demand. Let us consider then, the simple thing gold, separated from its native quartz, which we all know to be of limited supply and of use, hence, is of commercial value. We know its supply is uneven or variable, so is its demand for use ; hence, its commercial value is varied by change either in supply or demand, when there is not a corresponding change in the other.

But if its supply were always in the same ratio to, but less than its demand, its commercial value would remain fixed and unvariable. Now when gold was first employed as a medium of exchange unless its supply was simultaneously increased to exactly equal its increased demand for this new use, the value of the gold then in the control of man was immensely increased, and it was this increase of value which the law making gold a medium of exchange, gave to gold. The supply being the same the law gave it a new use, thereby adding a new value to it, and this is the only sense in which the law creates values, and yet, unaided by the law of personal interest of those needing a medium of exchange, that law could not add one particle to the value of the gold. If the law had the effect to increase the use, it increased the value; but those who make exchanges are the powers which decide whether a thing called money by law shall be used by entering into their transactions.

It is not necessary for us now to go into speculation as to what was first adopted by man as a measure of value and medium of exchange, or what improvements in the machinery of commerce led to the displacement of that by another and that by still another and another, until it has arrived to the materials now most generally in use, as silver, gold and paper securities, which we call paper money. Undoubtedly the adaptability of each article employed over those which preceded it, led to its adoption in its time, and that none of them has been universally and singly employed for any considerable length of time, is abundant proof that none has thus far been free of objections. And as it is easier to state a case actually existing than to imagine and state one parallel to it, I will leave the dead past to bury its dead and use existing facts and examples to base my further observations upon.

To-day in this country, as in Great Britain and many other countries, gold is adopted as the material possessing commercial value, best fitted for use as a standard measure of the values of all other articles of commerce. Silver preceded gold in this use, and is still the standard in many countries and in nearly all is used as a medium of exchange. We have also what we call minor coins or base metal currency, all of which possess in themselves intrinsic value but in widely varying degrees. Notwithstanding the difference in intrinsic value of these several species of coins from gold down, each and every one passes current at its nominal value and equally assist in proportion to their nominal value in facilitating exchanges and measuring values.

Now does not this seem paradoxical in view of the facts which we have noticed? Yet the fact is easily explained. Gold has an intrinsic and commercial value, resulting from i's limited supply and its use in the arts and in money. The people have declared through their laws that 23.22 grains of pure gold coined into a dollar piece of 25.8 grains shall be the unit of value. And to make the commercial value of all the coined money equal to its nominal value, the government coins all the metal money, issues it to the people at its nominal value in exchange for services or other things of commercial value, and agrees by its laws to redeem the silver and minor coins in gold coin of the standard value.

There is then this distinction between gold coin and all the rest. Gold coin carries with it only that value which is determined by the law of supply and demand for the gold in it, while each of the other coins carries with it not only the value determined by the supply and demand of the material in it, but the value of a credit which is attached to it to equal . the difference between its otherwise commercial value and that of its nominal value in gold. This fact, that silver and the minor coins pass current among the people at their nominal value equally with gold coin is cited by another school of political economists as an overwhelming proof that it is the law that gives money its value, and hence all that the law-making power needs to do to make good valuable current money is to say a thing shall be money without condition or restriction, and it will become so, and possessing whatever value the law prescribes, but believe me, nothing can be more chimerical.

It *does prove* that credit is an article of commerce, and when credit is of that quality that it is in equal supply and demand as gold coin, it will be of equal commercial value. If the law-makers could create money and affix its commercial value by the simple word and act of stamping an otherwise valueless thing, without any pledge or guarantee to preserve and maintain that value, it could practically annul the inexorable law of supply and demand, by supplying such money to an unlimited amount while there is a limited demand.

But what is credit ? Webster defines it as expectation of future payment for property transferred or promises given. History leads us to believe that the compounding the value of a credit with the value of a piece of metal coined into money as a medium of exchange was not known to the ancients but is of comparative modern invention, which was like every other invention the fruit of necessity. As commerce has grown among men, the medium of exchange has been improved to

meet its increased demand, and for the same reason we have at this age of the world another kind
of medium of exchange carrying with it practically
nothing of commercial value except that of credit ;
I speak of paper money.

Paper money was invented to answer a demand
of commerce almost as imperative as that which
led to the invention of money in its primitive
form. A need existed for an increased facility for
making exchanges, which the money then in use,
and the material of which it was made was in-
adequate in supply, and silver and gold exhausted
the list of known commodities possessing in themselves commercial value and the other necessary
requirements of money, such as divisibility, porta-
bility and durability, and when commerce had out-
grown these commodities in their use for money,
necessity pointed to credit, or paper money. Now
as I am discussing *facts*, let me analyze paper
money and see on what actual existing facts its
utility is founded. We all know it has utility, for it
is in use, and reason tells us if it were not sustained
by pre-existing facts, it could not so admirably
answer the purpose for which it was invented.

It is admitted by all logicians to be a self-evident
fact, that two things which are each equal to a

third are equal to each other and it is a fundamental rule of law that whatsoever a man does by his agent or representative he does by himself. Credit we have seen is the expectation of future payment for property transferred or promises given. That is credit in its commercial sense, and in the sense in which it is used in money. A piece of current paper money as you all know bears upon its face a promise to pay a certain sum of money. Now to what does that promise relate? Does it mean that the one who issued it agrees to pay it by giving another like it in exchange for that? By no means. It is an engagement on the part of the one who issued it with the holder, that on demand of the holder, he will redeem it by giving in exchange for it something which has in itself intrinsic and commercial value, equal to its face as compared with the standard unit of value.

It is the faith that the people have in the fulfillment of this promise, which gives this form of money its commercial value. The credit is founded upon the knowledge or belief that the one who made the promise is and will be able to fulfill it, and will do so on demand.

This paper then is the representative or agent of the value of the thing which secures its payment.

It is equal in value to the thing which is pledged for it, for it is exchangeable for it. We have next to see how its value is determined.

I have said that a gold dollar piece is by law the unit of value. We determine the value of paper money by comparing the value of the thing which secures it with the unit of value. Then it is clear that if we find that the security can be exchanged for the unit of value, to equal the face value of the piece of paper money which it secures, the paper money and the unit of value must be equal in commercial value.

Thus far I have spoken of money, when left subject only to the commercial law, except the adoption of a peculiar unit of value in this country. Had this unit not been fixed by the National law, it or some other would have been adopted by commercial law, and it is of national importance that it should be well known and universally conformed to that it has been so established.

It is of equally national importance that the money of the country should be equal in value throughout the country, for the obvious reason that it is or carries with it the measure of commercial value.

For these reasons, our forefathers in erecting

this republic, imposed on the National legislature the power to coin money, regulate the value thereof and of foreign coin and fix the standards of weights and measures, and prohibited to the States the right to make anything but gold and silver a legal tender.

From that time at least, nothing has been money which has not been made so by the highest law in the land ; for the power to issue money was not only vested, but exclusively vested in the National Government, and now all symbols of money, which have not been legalized by the government, are spurious, and subject those using it to severe penalties.

Great power over money is thus centralized in the government, and centralization of power is centralization of responsibility.

Is our money system perfect ? Verily no ! For want of the exercise of rightful authority over it, our system, while it is in some points in advance of the old, still lacks in a few of the most vital essentials. First, it is a *variable* measure of value. Second, its supply is delegated to private persons or corporations whose personal interests alone regulate its supply, and hence is never supplied to meet the just demands of the commerce of the country.

I believe you will all now agree with me that money is the measure of commercial values, and that that measure ought also to be the medium of exchange, and that in every system of measure there must be a unit of that measure, hence, there should be a unit of value, to which the value of all the measures of value should be made to relate and conform. This is simply admitting that so far our present money system is correct. We have an established unit of value and the value of all the other money of the country is made to equal the value of that unit in proportion to its nominal value. So far, so good. But here let me ask, what regulates the value of our unit of value, the gold dollar? I have the true answer to that question. It is the same law of supply and demand which regulates the value of every other article of commerce.

With a given supply the use of money has been greater at one time than another; and with a given supply, we have seen a variation in use creates a variation in value; and also that with a given use a variation in supply creates a variation in value. You are all so familiar with the expressions " money is scarce," " money is plenty," " money is worth 4 per cent.," " money is worth 12 per cent.," that I need not go into elaborate illustration of this point.

Money has two legitimate functions, the need of which brought it into being, and which ought to govern it even at the sacrifice of every other consideration. Those are, a medium of exchange, and a measure of value. To perform these functions, it should always be stable, unvariable and fixed in value, to secure which it must always be supplied in uniform proportion to its demand. When have these objects been attained? Never! Never! *Never!*

The only gauge we have by which we can determine the relative value of money one day from another, is the rate of interest it will bring in the money market, and unless you can point me to a period in the history of the world when money would draw a certain fixed unvariable rate of interest, day after day, month after month, and year after year, you cannot point me to an unvariable measure of value. You cannot do it. On the contrary, this first essential in all commercial transactions is and has always been most highly sensitive to the law of supply and demand, and in the power of Shylock, the extortioner, has been a merciless weapon applied to the back of toiling humanity, and has time out of mind raised the vagrant or base robber to the exalted estate of a king and debased the royal worker to the estate of a slave. That which was invented as a helper in the struggle of humanity for earthly existence has been left unprotected from the evil influences of improper control until it has, not from its nature but from its control, been stigmatized, the root of all evil.

Am I not stating facts? Do not the evils exist? Is there no *need* of improvement in our money system?

If there is need, who can say *that* need cannot be supplied? I pray you, pardon my seeming presumption when I assert that the evils which I have mentioned *do* exist, and that their remedy *is* within our reach.

While gold coin is the material adopted for the unit of value, its coinage should be unlimited by statute law, except the government should superintend or perform the work to guard against fraud. This is the case now, so no new law is needed on this point.

A silver-dollar-piece could be made the standard unit of value and was so until 1873, and perhaps with quite as much reason and beneficial results as the one now in use, but whatever material is used for that purpose, should be restricted in its amount of coinage by the demands of commerce alone. In the very nature of things two units of value cannot be used any more than two units of length ; with gold coin as a standard, commercial convenience should be the consideration governing the issue of the other coins or money, carrying with it all or a part of the value on which its currency is based. This again is about the state of that branch of the currency to-day.

Government should issue paper money based upon pledges or security in its control to supply all the demands of commerce not supplied by the kinds of money which I have mentioned, gold, silver and the minor coins. Does it do so ? Not altogether. Yet it does so to a sufficient extent to prove that it is possible to do so to *exactly* a sufficient extent.

The Government can issue its own notes upon its own credit so long as its own credit represented by its notes is at par with the unit of value. We have an example of this species of money in the Treasury note and United States notes commonly called greenbacks.

If commerce should need more paper money

than the resources of the National Government were sufficient to secure or more than its expenditures would enable it to put into circulation, for value received by it, it should provide other means of securing it and of getting it into circulation, for a valuable consideration.

Now has it provided such a means and such a currency? We have a kind of paper money, issued by the authority of the government, having its credit based on pledges of private property, (the value of which however, is the value of the Nation's credit,) National Bank Notes, but it is neither issued by the Government for value received, nor issued to the people in quantities to meet the demands of commerce. It is issued to private corporations practically free of charge, and by those corporations issued to the people not to meet the just needs and demands of commerce, but to meet the demands of the corporations. They are private institutions, having no motive in supplying money to commerce except that of their personal private interest which they nourish through the gains they make in manipulating the supply of money.

This system is objectionable for the reasons that it amounts to a free gift by the Government of an invaluable franchise to that class of citizens who are least in need of it, and that it places every commercial interest at the disposal of that class, to the infinite disadvantage of all the rest of the community.

Now if the interposition of these corporations was necessary, which I positively deny, they should be restrained from manipulating the supply of money, by guarding the measure of value against variability, and making it a necessity that they should consult and meet the just demands of commerce, in order to secure their highest personal interests.

This most desirable end can be accomplished by fixing the rate of interest which money of any and every description may draw.

Variability in the rate of interest for the use of money, is the bane of commerce, the silent engine used to bring about commercial revulsions and disaster the world over and for all past time. The commercial value of money is indicated by the rate of interest it draws. Interest is the price paid for the use of money, and the value of money is shown by the rate of interest it draws. Is this a contradiction of my assertion that the value of money is governed by the law of supply and demand? Not in the least; rather, interest shows you the degree of the supply and demand of money, that is all, and when the rate of interest changes, you know by that, that the ratio between supply and demand has been changed also.

Now it is clear that when persons or corporations whose business it is to furnish money for commerce by lending it to the people, and they have the money, and do not lend it, it is because they ask more for the use of it than is profitable to others. If they stint the supply they can get the more in proportion for what they supply, so that with a small security and scant supply of money, with high rate of interest they can make as much gain as with large security, ample supply of money and low interest.

To the thinking, reasoning mind every-day life in the commercial world discloses the wickedly vicious working of this system. It is through a vicious, variable rate of interest, that those who effect corners in money reap their unjust gains. We all know that corners in wheat, corn, butter and any of the necessaries of life are ruinous to the many and profitable to the few.

But since money is the measure of the values of all other commercial articles, a corner in it affects every other article of commerce by changing its commercial value to suit the value of money.

So, I say, it is the duty of Government, who authorizes the issue of money, to regulate its value by fixing the rate of interest it may draw when loaned for use, and fix it so securely that it cannot and will not be changed.

A few will object that it would be a violation of unalienable rights for Government to pass a law imposing a penalty on any one for lending his money as cheaply or as dearly as he pleased and could. They do not object so much to a penalty for lending money for *more* than a certain rate, principally, I suppose, because there have nearly always been laws with a view to that effect, but they say, it would be absurd, *outrageous*, to say that a man should not be permitted to lend his money to a poor fellow who was not able to pay more, or the legal rate, for as low a rate as he pleased. " Why " say they, " that would practically prohibit acts of charity !" These are the main objections raised to a fixed, unvariable rate of interest, and are raised by those engaged in the unholy traffic, to conceal their real motives, or by those who are blind to the most gigantic evil that ever oppressed mankind.

It is not the small capitalist who creates a corner in money. It is not he who vouchsafes to or withholds life from commerce, but I hold that all laws relating to money or anything of such general importance, should be general, and should be enacted with a view of accomplishing the greatest good to the greatest number, and who will deny that if fixing the rate of interest on money would secure us stability in the measure of value, its advantages would be immensely greater than its disadvantages ?

Let me show you then how it would accomplish that end, supposing Government should fix the legal rate of interest at three per cent. per annum — to be no more and no less.

If gold was worth less than three per cent. in the arts, and as money in other countries, it would be coined into money. If more in the arts than in money it would leave the money and go into the arts ; this would leave the supply of gold money subject to the law of supply and demand of commerce and not to the will of the usurer.

When the demand for money exceeded the supply of gold coin, paper and other money would be issued to meet that demand. The commerce would suffer no loss by the withdrawal of the gold

from circulation, because credit or paper money
equal to gold coin in value would take the place of
gold coin. By fixing the rate of interest gold coin,
of which the unit of value is composed, may draw
as money, we fix its value as money, and by con-
fining paper money to the same rate we preserve
the equality in the value of the currency. This
too, would prevent corners in money, for the
simple reason, that those who would otherwise
corner it could gain no advantage by doing so
if they could, being compelled to lay out of the
use of their money while they withheld it from
circulation without enhancing its value, and it
would thus, be to the personal interest of those who
issued the money to provide all that was demanded by commerce at the legal rate. The more
they issued the more their profits would be, and
when we want anything which it is in the power of
another to give, and it is for his personal interest
to give it, we are assured that our wants will be
gratified ; now does any one still question the right
of Congress to fix such a rate of interest ? If so, I
will refer him to Article 1, Section 8, of the Constitution, where it is laid down that Congress shall
have power, not only to coin money, but regulate
the value thereof. Now, if it has the power to

regulate the value of money, should it not do so? And how can it do so without fixing an unvariable rate of interest? Is it not as necessary that the measure of value should be fixed and unvariable, as that the measure of length or weight shall be so fixed?

Now a few words as to who should issue the paper money. The founders of this Republic conferred on Congress the powers over the value of money, for the obvious purpose of protecting the measure of value from the mercenary manipulations of private persons or corporations. It conferred this power in the same article and section of the Constitution that it did the power over the standard of weights and other measures. When this power was conferred on Congress, with it was imposed the duty of wisely exercising that power ; to delegate that power to private persons or corporations, and leave it to the discretion of those persons or corporations how that power shall be exercised, is a base abdication of sovereign power.

The power that exercises the control of the supply of money, performs a sovereign function, the importance of which cannot be exaggerated. The very life of commerce is subject to it, and the abuse of that power has marked its path with fortunes wrecked, homes turned to sepulchres, and honest toilers, the noblest of God's handiwork, driven from thrift and comfort to penury, misery and despair.

Shall we the sovereign people of this country allow this work of destruction to go on? We, whose servants Congressmen are, shall we submit to the demands of Shylock for his pound of flesh, when by the power we have, we can cause Shylock to seek us for favor? Let the Government provide a supply of money, sufficient to meet the demands of commerce and at a fixed rate of interest, and compel all other money-lenders to conform to the same rate on penalty of forfeiting the whole amount illegally loaned, and that to the borrower, and we will have a money system so just and equitable, and a measure of value so unvariable and certain, that the commerce of the country will be regenerated in vigor, the cry of the unemployed will no longer be heard, and the chief of the forces which has forever been making the rich richer and the poor poorer, will have become harmless among men, and that which was designed to be the servant of man, will no longer be his oppressor.

A DIALOGUE

— BETWEEN —

A. and B. on the Money Question,
By A. H. LOW.

A.   What is your horse worth, B. ?

B.   One hundred dollars.

A.   What is one hundred dollars worth?

B.   Six dollars a year.

A.   What is a dollar worth ?

B.   Six cents a year.

A.   I do not mean what is its use worth.

B.   Well, its present worth is 23.22 grains of gold coined into a dollar-piece of 25.8 grains.

A.   But how do you know the worth of your gold dollar ?

B.   I know that its supply is less than its demand for use, because men are willing to return it and an addition of six per cent. for the use of it a year.

A.   What is money *used* for ?

B.   In making exchanges of labor and commodities.

A.   Is money used more in making exchanges than other things are ?

B. Yes, nearly as much as all of them.

A. Why is money given such a preference in making exchanges?

B. Because it is by law made the measure of value, and the value of everything for sale is compared with its value.

A. Oh. Ah! But B., how do you know your horse is worth one hundred dollars?

B. Well there are men in this country who need horses that have none, and when they have one hundred dollars, are willing to exchange it for a good horse like this; and there are men who have such horses who need what one hundred dollars will buy more than they need the horse, so they exchange.

A. But cannot a man get more than six dollars net profit out of the use of such a horse in one year?

B. Oh, certainly he can! It is a poor horse indeed, that would not net his owner six dollars in one year.

A. Then why is he not worth more than one hundred dollars?

B. There are several reasons — but all centre in one — the difference between supply and demand.

A. Supply and demand of what?

B. Supply of and demand for such horses as mine.

A. I thought the usefulness of a horse determined what its price should be.

B. Well, that has something, but not all, to do with it.

A. I wish you would explain.

B. Many things are immensely useful, that have no commercial value or *price* ; air, sunlight, water etc. are fair examples. These are indispensable and valuable, but priceless ; everybody is supplied with all he needs and that freely.

A. You said six dollars a year interest indicated the value of one hundred dollars I think?

B. It shows the commercial value of the use of that sum.

A. Then the interest it draws does not determine the intrinsic value of money or its security?

B. No. It shows the difference between the supply of and demand for *money*.

A. But would not the price paid for the use of a horse for a year show the difference between the supply of and demand for such horse?

B. Yes.

A. Would not six dollars then be a fair compensation for the use of a one-hundred-dollar horse for one year ?

B.   Oh no !

A.   Now it seems to me that if six dollars is the price of the use of one hundred dollars for a year, six dollars ought to be the price for the use of a one-hundred-dollar-horse for the same length of time.

B.   You seem to forget that the nature of the two are widely different.   Money is practically imperishable ; under the protection that law provides, money is capable of being used eternally, and may be as capable of drawing interest the last year as the first ; while a horse can live only a few years at most and with the best of treatment is soon incapable of earning his own food, so that what he profits his owner must be done quickly ; and then, his owner runs the risk of his dying or becoming disabled.   The money-lender has no such concern — furthermore, when a man pays for the use of a horse he generally pays in *money*, not in a certain part of a horse.

A.   Now let us talk about interest on money a little.

B.   Agreed, what can you tell me about it ?

A.   I am here to ask questions.

B.   All right, I am here to answer.

A.   I suppose the rate of interest is regulated by law on a basis of justice between man and man, is it not?

B.   You were never more mistaken.

A.   But do not all of the States have legal rates of interest?

B.   Yes, but those rates have but little effect on money-lending.

A.   What are they for then?

B.   When a debt becomes due, as a judgment of a Court for a sum of money, or a promise is made for the payment of money in future with interest and no rate of interest is mentioned, the law presumes that the legal rate is agreed upon.

A.   But what is usury? Some States at least have usury laws.

B.   Interest was once called usury, but as now used, usury means interest in excess of the legal rate. The penalty for usury is seldom severe enough to prevent it.

A.   Why so? I should think if Government could declare a legal rate of interest, it ought to be able to enforce it.

B.   So it should, but the money-lenders have a

good deal to do with making those laws and they leave room for evasion.

A.   But what need is there of any usury laws, or any laws on interest at all ? Why not leave everybody free to make their own bargains and let every case be governed by its peculiar circumstances ?

B.   Do you not remember that I told you, money is the measure of commercial value ? That being so, any change in its rate of interest indicates a change in its measuring capacity, whereas being a standard measure it ought to be unvariable.

A.   Your reasoning seems good, but if you are right all the rest of the world are wrong, are they not ? And if you say that, then you must be crazy or what we moderns call a crank.

B.   If this were not so serious a matter I would laugh at you. How many years has it been since a man was condemned and sentenced to have his head cut off, and, that too, by a high court of learned wise men (?) for saying that the earth revolved around the sun ? And yet to-day, one who denies it is almost as certain of being sent to an insane asylum. Age will not make a falsehood truth, neither will Truth down at sight of a host of opposition. The institution of money is purely a human invention, and if it don't work right as a system, there is no divine prohibition to our examining it, and if we can find a difficulty, we have a right and it is our *duty* to apply a remedy, if we can invent one.

A. Well, I notice that those who have the least money are generally those who find the most fault with our money system.

B. Your observation is correct, although I fear I detect sarcasm in your remark. May I ask you, do the well seek a physician? Do oppressors complain of oppression? Do our millionaires complain of a system or condition of things that enables them to multiply their riches year after year out of the earnings of millions of their fellow beings, and that too without the performance of an honest day's labor in a year? None but sufferers seek relief, and if their opponents cannot answer their questions and arguments, their only resort is further wrong, *or ridicule*, and I tell you, *hundreds of us will bear wrong where one will brave ridicule.*

A. You reply with considerable spirit. Do you really think there is any thing radically wrong with our money system?

B. Indeed, I know it, and not only ours, but that of every nation I know of on earth.

A. Ha, ha! Surely B., you must be provided with kind treatment in an asylum. But since you are so much in earnest, will you point out to me wherein the nations need regulating in their money systems ?

B. You want a six weeks' lecture condensed into three minutes I suppose, without anything left to be understood.

A. That's about it, and of course I don't expect to understand that, since you seem to be the only man on earth who can and does understand it.

B. You are quite in error about numbers. On the contrary there are but few people in the world who do not believe there is some evil of fearful power in money so much so that there is a proverb current among its victims, that " money is the root of all evil,'' but those who have plenty of money seldom quote the proverb. I have made it my business to investigate the matter to see if I can find what is wrong, and I think I have discovered it and invented a remedy. I do not claim, however, that I am alone in either the discovery or the invention. I have drawn largely from the opinions, learning and arguments of others, to any of whom

I am ready to ascribe superiority in everything but good intentions.

A. I must say you are very modest in your pretensions, but I am all ears for your theory, although I expect to find it a house built upon sand, or perhaps even in air, but I will do as well as I can to divest myself of my prejudices in favor of " the best money system in the world," while I listen to you.

B. Since you seem to be honest and willing to give me a fair chance, I proceed to give you such light as I am able. You will admit, I trust, that in every commercial country the money of that country is such as the law prescribes, and that different nations have different money. That there is nothing that is actually money the world over.

A. I am not so ready to agree with you. Take gold and silver, or gold alone, is not that money anywhere and everywhere ?

B. *No Sir.* Gold is pretty generally accepted in exchange for other commodities but it is always by weight when it is out of the country in which it was coined into money. A gold coin carries no legal power with it out of the country in which it was coined, unless the laws of the other country have expressly made it a legal tender.

A. What do you mean by that ?

B. ‹ By a legal tender I mean, that function which the law of a country adds to the material of which its money is made, so that a creditor is bound to take it when *tendered* in payment of his claim or else have nothing for it.

A. Well, is not gold a legal tender in this country ?

B. No, not until it is coined into money according to law.

A. Well, go on.

B. Since, then, the money of a nation is prescribed by and made according to the law of that nation, there must be a power somewhere to carry the law into execution, by doing that with the special commodity which will convert it into money, unless the law designates some commodity as a class for that purpose — which is not usual.

A. The government of each nation attends to the matter, I suppose.

B. That depends upon who the Government happens to be. Under a despotism or absolute monarchy undoubtedly the matter is attended to for the interests of the government, for it is among the most important prerogatives of sovereignty. No government can exist long after that prerogative has passed out of its control.

A. I suppose in a free country like this the same rule does not apply? Everybody is interested in the welfare of the Government.

B. In this country the people are the Government or at least our Constitution was established on that proposition, and if in an absolute monarchy, the prerogative of making or issuing the money is essential to the perpetuity of the Government, it follows that that prerogative should be as sacredly preserved in the Government representing the people of this country.

A. Well we are all right then, for Article 1, Section 8, of the Constitution provides that Congress shall have power to coin money, regulate the value thereof and of foreign coin, and fix the standard of weights and measures.

B. What good is that authority unless it is exercised?

A. But don't the Government coin all the money of this country?

B. By no means, I do not suppose you will confine the word coin to the forming and stamping of metal money. Whatever is made money is *coined* as much as tho' it were metal. Everything to be money must first be coined such.

A.   I don't think I will admit that.   A coin is a piece of metal money.

B.   But it was not money until coined ; coining it made it money ; it was metal only before, and since the Constitution provides for no other than coined money, we must swamp the Government on the construction of a word, for want of material to coin into metal money, or proceed to stamp other material and endow it with the properties of money and let the Government flourish.

A.   Well, there is lots of money in the country besides metal money, so we will not quarrel about that, but don't the Government make it all and regulate its value ?

B.   It does not.   The Government does coin all the metal money and a considerable of paper money, but a large proportion of our money is issued if not coined by private parties.   However, the *coinage* is not all the Constitution provides for ; Congress is to regulate the value of money and of foreign coins, and fix the standards of weights and *measures*.   Now since money is the measure of value, Congress should fix its standard as well as that of length.

A.   But has it not done so, in declaring 25.8 grains gold coin the unit of value ?

B. No sir. Do you think in fixing the stand-ard unit of weight, it would be sufficient to say it should be made ot brass ؛

A. You are not fair. The Government fixes the quantity of the gold dollar.

B. I admit that, but the Constitution says, Congress shall have power to regulate the *value*, not the quantity of money.

A. I think you are splitting hairs now. Is not a dollar a dollar as much one time as another ?

B. Oh yes, its name never changes, but its value does very often.

A. How do you make that out ?

B. By observation and by reasoning from first principles. You recollect that the commercial value of a thing depends upon the supply of and demand for it, and the value of money is as sensi-tive to that law as anything else, and I wish you to bear in mind, that it is the *commercial*, not the *in-trinsic* value of a thing that is determined by the law of supply and demand, at the same time the two are-inseparable in an article of commerce, for use is as essential an element in commercial value as in intrinsic value. Nothing that is useless, has commercial value. Now you know that the supply of, is not always in the same proportion to the demand for money. Hence I say its value changes.

A.   If that is so, how does the change in value manifest itself?

B.   By the change in the rate of interest charged and received by those whose business it is to lend money.

A.   How does it happen that the supply and demand vary so?

B.   It is due to the personal interest of those who issue and lend money.

A.   Do you mean to say that the commerce of the country, the rights of everybody are at the mercy of the personal interests of any private person or persons.

B.   That is it, sir.   There is a class of our citizens organized into what are called National Banking Associations, with special corporate rights and the principal of those rights is to supply money for the commerce of the country.

A.   Well of course they are so controlled by law as to produce the most desirable results for the people who have granted those rights?

B.   On the contrary, the private interests of those corporations are the only regulators in the matter of supplying much or little money.   If they can profit more by supplying much, they supply much. If more by supplying little, they supply but little.

A. But how do you account for such an abdication of sovereign power as you call it by the Government of this country? I can't· help but think you are mistaken.

B. There are two ways of accounting for it. The favored few corrupted our Congress to pass the law, or else our Congress was ignorant of the principles upon which money depends. Charity forbids the former idea, and pride of National wisdom is reluctant to admit the latter. Perhaps Congress acted upon the theory that these bankers would consider that their personal interests would be increased by increased welfare and prosperity of the people generally. Such an idea has no foundation in fact.

A. I am not convinced of that.

B. Well sir, money-lenders, like lawyers, doctors and wreckers, make their profits out of the misfortunes of others, and when the fortunes of others 'are so much in the power of their " helpers " as the people's are in the power of the money-lenders, especially the National Banking Associations, a blind man ought to be able to see which of the parties will get the lion's share.

A.   But how do other peoples' fortunes depend upon the pleasure of the money-lenders?   I think you are assuming too much.

B.   Will you admit that it is a misfortune for a man to be in debt and not able to pay?

A.   Most men feel happier out of it, at least I do.

B.   Well, suppose you were unfortunate enough to have to borrow money, and you borrowed a sum of money of a banker at six per cent. for one year. At the end of the year you wanted to renew your note another year.   You had as good security to give as you had before but could not pay the money back without a great sacrifice of property ; but on application you found the rate of interest to be twelve per cent. which was much more than the use of the money would return to you ; would you not consider yourself unfortunate, owing to the change of interest ?

A.   I should say I would.

B.   Well, the powers that supply the money work that change, and your misfortune is their gain.

A.   Well, is that all the trouble ; they don't hurt those who don't have to borrow money, do they ?

B.   Indeed they do. Their influence is as

general throughout the country as the heart's is on the body of a man.

A.   Now don't go to making poetry to me, keep down to facts, plain and simple if you have any.

B.   No better comparison could be made, but you shall have solid facts, for they are abundant. You are aware that the interest on money differs in different States ; and that money commands a higher rate of interest at one time than at another in the same State.   Debt and credit are so common in this country that there is scarcely any industry into the transactions of which they do not enter.   Those who do not borrow or lend money are scarce in this country, except among the poorest laboring class.   This to be sure comprehends the larger portion of the community.

A.   I am aware of all that.

B.   Contracts are made on a *money* basis.   Any change in the basis affects all such contracts. When money is paid on a contract previously made, and the money is worth more than it was when the contract was made, the one who pays it loses the difference, and *vice versa*.   The change may be so unexpected and violent that the debtor cannot meet it.   He may have thousands of men in his employ, whom he is compelled to discharge.   He becomes bankrupt, and they tramps. As a people we are dependent upon one another, and a system that works injustice to any, affects all, and when after a season of activity and thrift a " money panic " comes, the common laborer who lives from hand to mouth but never borrows money is the one who suffers most.

A. Well I confess you have answered my questions very clearly and perhaps I may as well admit that you have answered them correctly, but I fear you are like many other doctors, better informed as to the disease, than what will cure it. It is an undeniable fact that we Americans are becoming chronic grumblers, we grumble about everything from the weather to the " hard times." I hope you are an exception and will not show up our country's faults too badly without pointing out the way to mend them.

B. I am certainly able to do that, and since you are a good listener, it will afford me great pleasure to lay before you a perfect plan whereby we may cure the evil of our present money system.

The first thing I would advise would be that Congress exercise the power and perform the duty imposed on it in Section 8, of Article 1, of the Constitution, to fix the standards of measures or rather that of the measure of value, as well as the other standards.

A. Surely it has done so, for it has declared 23.22 grains of gold coined into a dollar-piece of 25.8 grains to be the unit of value.

B. So far so good, but what determines the value of the gold dollar ?

A. That is regulated by the law of supply and demand.

B. Exactly so ; then if its value is regulated by the law of supply and demand, Congress does not regulate it, as the Constitution says it shall " have power to coin money and regulate the value thereof."

A. I don't see what more Congress can do towards regulating the value of gold. What do you mean ? .-

B. Simply this. While the gold dollar is the unit of value, *its* value rises and falls whenever there is a change in supply or demand, unless there is a corresponding change in the other.

An increased supply without an increased demand, lessens the value.

An increased demand without an increased supply, increases the value.

A diminished supply without a diminished demand, increases the value.

A diminished demand without a diminished supply, lessens the value.

A change in both supply and demand not corresponding and proportional changes the value, and so since it is practically impossible for Congress to regulate the supply of gold it has but one way to regulate its value and that is by regulating its demand for use.

A.   It seems to me as impossible for Congress to regulate the demand as the supply of gold.   Please explain.

B.   It is easily done.   Gold is used as money, in this country by permission of Congress.   Congress has the power to demonetize it altogether. It was only in 1873 that the gold dollar was made the unit of value.   If Congress should demonetize gold in this country, it would lessen the use of a large quantity of gold as money and accordingly lessen the value of gold all over the world.   So you will see that if Congress can regulate its use as it surely can, it can by that very means regulate its value.

A.   I would like to hear your plan.

B.   I must first recall your attention to the

interest on money. You recollect that interest is the price paid for the *use* of money. Suppose we say three per cent. interest is a normal or just rate of interest at this time. Now if to-morrow men need money which they have not got, and they cannot get it short of five per cent. and they will give that, it shows that the money is worth more to-morrow than to-day does it not? and if the gold dollar is the unit of value it rises in value to meet the increased demand. My plan then is to prescribe the rate of interest at a fixed point, and provide paper money so secured as to be equal in value with gold, to meet any increased demand for money, over and above that rate, and in the same manner, if foreign exchanges or the arts call for gold so that its value would be increased by lessening the supply of money, I would issue paper money to take the place of that which is withdrawn from the currency. By this means we would have all the money we wanted at a fixed legal rate of interest and would counteract the influences of commerce in other countries and of speculators in their action upon the value of gold, our standard of value.

A. How would you supply the paper money so promptly and regularly?

B. The Government should attend to the issue

of that just as it does to the issue of metal money, and further, I would have the Government establish loan offices all over the country, wherever needed, and lend its notes to the people on demand, by their giving good security for it, and that it should always be loaned at a fixed rate of interest. I would also have the Government declare its notes money, and a full legal tender.

A. That might do to get money out into circulation, but how about contracting it when commerce did not need it?

B. Whenever money would not be worth the legal rate of interest it would show that there was too much in circulation and those who had borrowed of the Government would pay back their loans and take up their securities.

A. But it seems to me that your plan would favor the rich by giving those who had securities to put up the only chance to borrow money.

B. Would it do so any more than the present system? Can a poor man get money at our banks now? You will see I do not propose to lend money to anybody free of charge as the Government does to the National banks now. Those who have property to give as security won't borrow money and pay interest on it and then lock it up in their safes. When they borrow it, it will be to use it and that means that they will buy property with it or employ laborers to work in some of the fields of industry, and that means activity in commerce, and that means general prosperity.

A.   But why should Government charge interest on its loans, to the people. It seems to me that if the Government could lend money in that way it could do it at least for what it cost to keep up the loan offices and print the notes.

B.   For Government to loan to the rich or those who could put up security alone, and that without charge, would be a great wrong, one of the wrongs I seek to stop ; for now the Government is doing practically that for the National Banks, who pay for the Government indorsement only a small tax to pay the cost of printing notes, etc. There are two good reasons why Government should charge interest.

First. If Government should issue money free of cost to all who applied money would soon lose all its value. It is only from the fact that there is a difference between supply and demand that anything has commercial value.

Second. The Government is a part of or representative of everybody. The use of money is valuable and it would be unjust for Government to lend money to one without a consideration and not to all alike, and if everybody could get money of the Government by the asking, the money would soon lose its value. No one would exchange his property for the money of another when he could get the same amount of money of the Government for nothing. Again if the borrower of the Government was required to pledge the title to his property for the loan and was still permitted to enjoy the use of the property and paid nothing for the use of the money, there would be no inducement for him to return the money, and the man who had the most property to pledge in that way could get the most favor from the Government — just the injustice I am trying to check.

Again — the credit of the United States is the common stock of all, and whoever draws from that stock should leave an equivalent for that which he gets, which equivalent belongs to all in common.

Can you understand my theory now?

A. I do, or let me see — you advocate a fixed and uniform rate of interest. That the Government should always stand ready to lend money at that rate. That all money should be issued by the Government whether metal or paper, and that the volume of the money should be regulated by the demands of commerce alone, and the value of it regulated and fixed by the law of the country.

B. You have it, sir, to a dot, which shows me you have been an attentive listener for which I sincerely thank you.

A. I am as thankful to you, for you have taught me to think, and not to be led by partisans nor driven with a party whip.

Hereafter I shall advocate the Common Sense System of Finance.

NOTE.—The Author cordially invites public and private criticism.

"The laborer is worthy of his hire." *Luke x. 7.*

www.ingramcontent.com/pod-product-compliance
Lightning Source LLC
Chambersburg PA
CBHW031444270326
41930CB00007B/855